STUDIUM BIBLICUM FRANCISCANUM

GUIDES

— 1—

Stanislao Loffreda

# RECOVERING
# CAPHARNAUM

Second Edition

Franciscan Printing Press
Jerusalem
1993

'Rabbi, where do you live?'
'Come and see' he replied;
so they went and saw
where he lived...
(John 1:38-39)

# Index

Frontispiece: General view of Capharnaum.
1. Potsherd with a cross.
2. Reconstructed window of the
synagogue.

# *Preface*

This archaeological guide aims at providing a short but reliable and up-to-date summary of nineteen seasons of excavations (1968-1986) conducted in Capharnaum by Fr. Virgilio C. Corbo and by the writer. These are the imposed limits of the booklet.

We archaeologists are excavating the material remains of the past, but we are looking for something more. Our final goal is to meet again the past generations, to speak with them and let them speak to the present generations. "The archaeologist, as M. Wheeler used to say, is digging up not things, but people".

When we keep in mind that Capharnaum was "the town of Jesus" and in some way the cradle of Christianity, we may soon realize that the unearthed remains are of a tremendous significance for mankind. If these pages help you to meet the inhabitants of ancient Capharnaum, many of whom you know already by their names, our goal is fully accomplished.

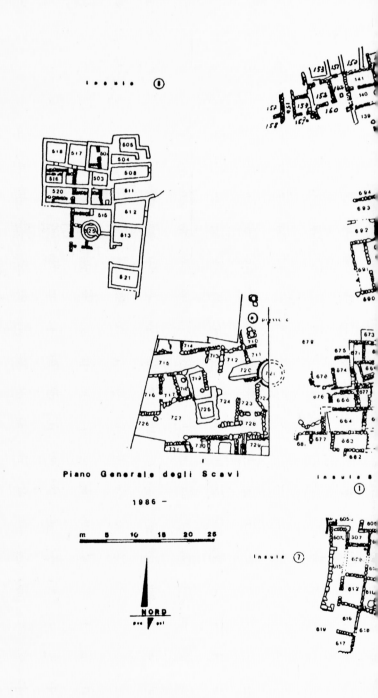

Piano Generale degli Scavi

1986 –

m   5   10   15   20   25

NORD

# 3. General plan of the ruins (1986).

# CAPHARNAUM REDISCOVERED

## 1. Surveys and Excavations

The archaeological site, called at present Kefar Nahum in Hebrew and Talhum in Arabic, is located on the NW shore of lake Kinneret in Galilee some 210 m below sea level, 16 km from Tiberias, 3 km from et-Tabgha and 5 km from the upper Jordan river.

The biblical site, though at some distance from modern settlements, can be easily reached both by land through an asphalt road encircling the lake, and by boats leaving from Tiberias and from En Gev.

The ancient village was abandoned a millennium ago, but some Arab families of the Semekiyeh tribe kept living there until the Arab-Israeli war of 1948. Two thirds of the ruins

4. Lintel of the synagogue.
5-6. Capharnaum can be reached both by land and by boat.
7. The prostrate ruins of the synagogue before 1905.

belong to the Franciscan Custody of the Holy Land, while the remainder on the east side belongs to the Greek-Orthodox Patriarchate.

The American scholar E. Robinson, who visited the site in 1838, left the following description: "The whole place is desolate and mournful. A few Arabs only of the Semekiyeh were here encamped in tents, and had built up a few hovels among the ruins which they used as magazines". Not far from the lake shore Robinson noticed "the prostrate ruins of an edifice which, for expense, labour and ornament, surpasses any thing we have yet seen in Palestine". During a second visit he correctly identified that building as a synagogue.

The English archaeologist C. W. Wilson in 1866 made in the synagogue a small sounding, which was still insufficient to provide a reliable plan of the edifice. Further, he described two monumental tombs, one of which is still visible some 200 m north of the synagogue.

11

In the following years the precious remains of the synagogue were heavily damaged by local Bedouins and by the inhabitants of Tiberias. This pitiable destruction, deplored in vain by the French traveller Guérin (1880), continued until 1894. In that year the Franciscan Custody of the Holy Land, through brother Giuseppe Baldi of Naples, acquired from the Bedouins the ruins of the synagogue and a large area of ancient Capharnaum. The Franciscan property was soon fenced off and protected by stone walls still visible today; and even the remains of the synagogue were carefully covered with earth for further protection against any vandalism.

In 1905 Kohl and Watzinger of the Deutsche Orient-Gesellschaft were allowed by the Franciscans to excavate the synagogue. The cleaning of that imposing monument was continued in the following years (1906-1915) by the Franciscan architect Brother Wendelin von Menden, who excavated also a portion of the ancient village on the W and SW sides of the synagogue, and finally started the excavations of an octagonal church some 30 m S of the synagogue.

In 1921 Fr. Gaudentius Orfali of Nazareth, conducted a short season of excavations, partly uncovering the octagonal church and exposing an Arab level of the town in the area between the synagogue and the octagonal church. To this young Franciscan we owe the restoration of the synagogue. A long dedicatory inscription in Latin was engraved on one column of the N stylobate by the Department of Antiquities to commemorate the event. After Orfali's untimely death in 1926, no major work was done in Capharnaum for some 40 years.

From 1968 to 1991 the dynamic Franciscan archaeologist Fr. Virgilio C. Corbo and the writer worked almost without interruption in rediscovering ancient Capharnaum. The excavations concentrated first on the two public buildings of the town, namely on the octagonal church and on the synagogue; and our efforts were rewarded by the sensational discovery of the house of St. Peter and of the first century synagogue built by the Roman centurion. In addition, a large portion of the ancient village was brought to light, clarifying the long and fascinating history of the site. Fr. Corbo continued the reconstruction of the synagogue and completely reshaped the Franciscan property to cope with the ever increasing number of pilgrims and tourists. He died on Dec. 6, 1991 and he was buried in the insula sacra under the modern Church which had been dedicated on June 29, 1990.

In the meantime Dr. V. Tzaferis of the Department of Antiquities conducted five seasons of excavations in the Greek-Orthodox property (1978-1982).

## 2. The name

The original Semitic name of the settlement is Kefar Nahum i.e. the village (kafar) of Nahum (personal name). It is not possible to identify this Nahum after whom the village was named. Some ancient writers bypassed the problem of identification since they took Nahum as a common noun. For instance, Origen interpreted Kefar Nahum as "the village of consolation" from the etymological meaning of the Hebrew root nhm (consolation); whereas St. Jerome in some cases translated the same name as "the beautiful city", from the Hebrew root n'm (beauty).

The composite name Kefar Nahum is always rendered in non-Semitic languages as a single name, and the guttural h has been dropped altogether. In the Greek manuscripts of the Gospels two spellings occur, i.e. Capharnaum (Καφαρναούμ) and Capernaum (Καπερναούμ). The first transcription "Capharnaum", closely following the Hebrew pronunciation

14

and adopted also by Josephus Flavius, is the right one, while the spelling "Capernaum" is rather an idiom of the district of Antioch.

Apparently the old Semitic name Kefar Nahum was still in use even after the village had been deserted. In fact the Jewish traveller Ishak Chelo (1333) writes: "from Arbel we reached Kefar Nahum, which is the Kefar Nahum of our sages".

Two centuries later, however, the ruins are called Tanhum. Uri of Biel (1537) writes: "Tanhum. Here rabbi Tanhum is buried". Most probably the presumed tomb of R.Tanhum gave the new name to the ruins. In a parallel way, the biblical town of Bethany near Jerusalem was renamed el-Arariyeh in Arabic, from the Lazarium, i.e. the tomb of Lazarus. The local Bedouins pronounced the new name Tanhum as Talhum, changing n in l. The spelling, recorded for the first time by Fr. Michel Nau (1668) is still in use.

Finally several travellers and archaeologists misinterpreted Talhum as Tell Hum, i.e. "the ruin" (tell) of Nahum - the initial n being dropped.

## 10a. Capharnaum from the Mountain of the Beatitudes.

## 3. Identification of ancient Capharnaum

The identification of the ruins of Talhum with ancient Capharnaum was not accepted unanimously by the topographers of the nineteenth century; in fact, several scholars identified Capharnaum with Kh. Minyeh, a ruin in the Ginnosar valley due S of Tell 'Oreimeh and 14 km from Tiberias.

Today, after the excavations of both Talhum and Kh. Minyeh, and after a better knowledge of literary sources, the identification of ancient Capharnaum with Talhum is no longer a matter of dispute. To start with, the ruins of Kh. Minyeh turned out to be simply an Omayyad castle, and no pre-Arab remains were found. To the contrary, the excavations of Talhum brought to light all the periods of occupation recorded by literary sources. Besides, the two public buildings of Talhum, i.e. the synagogue and the house of St. Peter, fit the descriptions of the pilgrims. Finally the ruins of Talhum exactly match the geographical setting of ancient Capharnaum; in fact, they are located two miles from Heptagegon-Tabgha (Theodosius), two miles from Korazin (Eusebius), and between Heptapegon and the upper Jordan river.

# THE VILLAGE

## 1. Description

The ruins of ancient Capharnaum cover approximately an area of 6 hectares (60,000 square m). The village stretched for about 300 m from E to W along the lake shore, the easternmost limits being in the area where the Greek-Orthodox church is built, and for some 200 m from S to N, i.e. from the lake shore to the hills.

In the maximum expansion during the Byzantine period, Capharnaum could easily number some 1,500 inhabitants. Any assessment of the population is still premature as far as the other periods of occupations are concerned. To be sure, Capharnaum was by far inferior to the large cities of the lake; for example, according to Josephus Flavius, Magdala held a population of more than 40,000 persons during the first Jewish war. Yet, the village enjoyed a privileged position, its economic resources being fishing, agriculture, industry and trade. To start with, Capharnaum was a border-town provided with customs (Mc 2:13-15) along the main imperial highway leading to Damascus. It was also the only settlement on the NW shore of the lake, 5 km from the upper Jordan river which marked the border between the Tetrarchy of Herod Antipas and the Golan across the river assigned to Philip.

Most probably the imperial highway bypassed the N flank of the village; in fact some 100 m NE of the synagogue and close to a monumental mausoleum a milestone was found in 1975 bearing the following inscription:

IMPERATOR
CAESAR DIVI
TRAIANI PARTHICI
FILIUS DIVI NERVAE
NEPOS - TRAIANUS
ADRIANUS AUGUSTUS...
"The Emperor
Caesar of the divine
Traianus Particus
son - of the divine Nerva
nephew, Traianus
Adrianus Augustus..."

Capharnaum was commercially linked in a prominent way with the northern regions, i. e. upper Galilee, Golan, Syria, Phoenicia, Asia Minor and Cyprus. This conclusion is based on the study of the coins and of the imported vessels so far found in Capharnaum. To the contrary, contacts with central and southern Palestine were surprisingly scanty.

The presence of a detachment of Roman soldiers at Capharnaum (Lc 7: 1-10; Mt 8: 5-13) stresses the importance of the village as a crossroad for many travellers leaving and entering the Tetrarchy of Herod Antipas. Besides, Capharnaum controlled at least 8 km of the lake shore, from the springs called

today et-Tabgha to the upper Jordan river. Even today this side of the lake is particularly rich for fishing. It is perhaps not by chance that many disciples of Jesus were fishermen. It is also significant that Peter and his brother Andrew left their hometown Bethsaida across the lake and settled in Capharnaum as a more fitting place for their fishing activity.

Agriculture was highly developed. Excavations have brought to light olive presses, grinding stones for wheat and cereals, mortars, stone bowls and craters etc. These tools mostly of basalt stones were made in Capharnaum itself, as can be proved by several unfinished pieces; and they were considered as a precious family heritage. Another industrial activity of the village was the manufacture of glass vessels.

An appreciable portion of the ancient village has been excavated since 1968, providing an insight to the living quarters. The private houses so far excavated are rather unpretentious but by no means poor, al least according to the living standard of an ancient village. They also betray no sharp economic differentiation. Local volcanic basalt stones in their natural state were used to build walls and pavements. Walls were built without true foundations, and the one storey rooms could

hardly reach more that 3 m in height, judging from several staircases leading to the roof. Fairly regular courses were levelled with small pebbles and soil, but with no help of strong mortar, at least in the Hellenistic and Roman periods; even in the Byzantine period mortar was employed only in some cases, and not as a rule.

Light roofs made up of wooden beams and of beaten earth mixed with straw covered the squat rooms, and they were reached from open courtyards through a flight of stone steps.

The private houses consisted of several units following a fairly standard pattern with minor differences; several roofed rooms clustered around a large open courtyard. Actually the open courtyard was the focal point of a house. Its conspicuous size in comparison to the small roofed rooms was dictated by the climatic conditions of Capharnaum where in summertime the temperature lingers around 35 degrees. The squat roofed rooms received light from a series of windows facing the inner courtyard. They were used as shelters, for sleeping at least in the rainy season, and as a place where the inhabitants kept their belongings; whereas many daily life activities took place in the courtyard. Grinding stones and ovens for instance are always found in the courtyard. Here women fixed the meal; here the artisans worked and probably here too people used to sleep in the summertime on stretched mats on the floor.

Hygienic facilities, such as wash-rooms, drainage systems etc., did not exist. Neither can we find in Capharnaum water cisterns as in

16. Olive press.
17. Handmills.
18. Glass vessels from Capharnaum.

Korazin, or underground silos as in Nazareth. The proximity of the lake is responsible for this lack. A house of this kind with many roofed rooms around a common courtyard entered from the public street through a single doorway, most probably was shared by two or more kindred families living in a patriarchal fashion.

Not all the buildings of the village follow this standard pattern; several structures were uncovered along the E side of a large NS street flanking the synagogue where the characteristic hovens and stone steps set in the large courtyards are missing. Most probably many of these units facing the main street of the village are to be interpreted as shops.

The general layout of the houses by no means conveys an image of a haphazard rural settlement; to the contrary, we can visualise a large village where merchants, artisans, farmers and fishermen built their dwellings according a harmonious plan. The main streets run in a NS direction and are intersected at right angles by small alleys, in a Hellenistic-Roman pattern of "cardo maximus" and "decumani". Finally the intersection of the NS streets and the EW alleys created several blocks or city-quarters which we call "insulae".

20. Isometric view of insula n. 2.
21. Courtyard of a private house of insula n. 2.

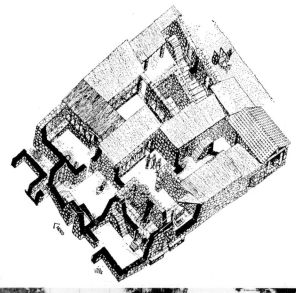

22. A series of windows in insula n. 2.
23. General view of insula n. 6.

# 2. Periods of Occupation

The archaeological remains of Capharnaum cover a period of at least three thousand years, from 2000 B.C. to 1000 A.D. in round numbers. Besides, Palaeolithic flints give a dating of several thousand years before the Christian era. Early third millennium sherds (bend-slip ware) show that the site was occasionally visited by man in the crucial period when urban life developed in the Holy Land (Early Bronze Age). Walls and pavements of second millennium B.C. (Middle and Late Bronze) were found Instead, no trace of occupation has been found so far covering the long Israelite period (1200 - 587 B.C.).

The fifth century B.C. marks the beginning of a very long an continuous period of occupation, several remains of which have been found under the synagogue, under the octagonal church, in insula n. 2 and particularly on the area immediately to the west. This we believe is the nucleus of the Persian period settlement from which Capharnaum spread in all directions in the following centuries. Of course Capharnaum was not born as a full-fledged town, but developed gradually. In due time old houses were completely replaced by new ones, or in other cases old walls were reinforced while new stone pavements were added. Up to now we have no clear indication that during the Roman and Byzantine periods the village underwent a wholesale and drastic destruction due to wars of physical calamities. Even the traumatic transition to the Arab period in the seventh century A.D. was not marked by a sudden and global distruction: apparently several houses of the village were simply abandoned, while other units continued in use well into the Arab period. Under the Ommayad rulers of Damascus the site was fully reoccupied; but during this period the synagogue and the octagonal church were abandoned for good. During the Abassid dynasty of Bagdad Capharnaum prosperity declined sharply. Some structures were built in Capharnaum in the 12-13th cent. A.D., but the village as such was by that time a pile of ruins.

25. Lintel of the synagogue.
26. Capital with menorah.

## 3. The Inhabitants

St. Epiphanius informs us that until the fourth century A.D. the population of Capharnaum was entirely Jewish: "This praxis, forbidding any one of a different race to live among them (i. e. among the Jews) is particularly followed in Tiberias, in Diocaesarea (i. e. Sepphoris), in Nazareth and in Capharnaum". On the other hand, some passages of the Mishna stress that the Jewish population of Capharnaum during the first three centuries of the Christian era formed two distinct and antagonistic blocks: Orthodox Jews, and Minim or heretics. From the

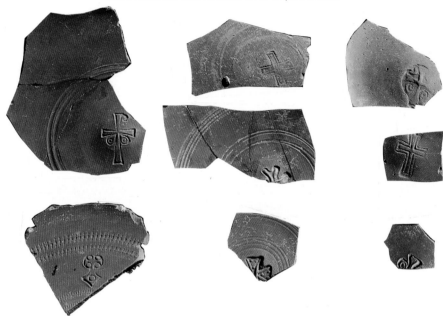

context it is clear that those Minim of Capharnaum were Jews converted to Christianity, i. e. Jewish-Christians.

Already before the second Jewish Revolt of 135 A.D. this Jewish-Christian community of Capharnaum had reached even the high sphere of Orthodox Judaism by converting to the sect rabbi Hanina, the nephew of the famous rabbi Jehoshua. "Hanina, son of the brother of Jehoshua, came to Kephar Nahum, and the Minim worked a spell on him, and set him riding on a ass on the Sabbath. He came to Jehoshua his friend, and he put ointment on him and he was healed. He (R. Jehoshua) said to him: Since the ass of that wicked one (i. e. Jesus) has roused itself against thee,

thou canst no longer remain in the land of Israel. He departed thence to Babel, and he died there in peace" (Midrash Qoh Rabba I:8).

Two centuries later between the end of the third and the first decades of the fourth century, the Jewish Christians of Capharnaum had substantially increased to the point that Rabbi Issi of Caesarea cursed the inhabitants of the village. "Rabbi Issi of Caesarea explained this verse in reference to Minuth...Good is Hananijah, nephew of R. Jehoshua; bad is the population (ad litteram: the sons) of Kefar Nahum" (Midrash Qoh Rabba VII: 26).

We cannot jump to the conclusion that all the inhabitants of Capharnaum were Minim at that time. On the other hand R. Issi could not pass this heavy sentence against "the sons of Capharnaum" if the Minim constituted just an insignificant segment of that village.

It is difficult to tell when exactly and to what extend the Gentile-Christians (i.e. Christians converted from the gentiles) supplanted the Jewish-Christian community of Capharnaum. There is however no reasonable doubt that the mid-fifth century octagonal church was built by Gentile-Christians.

In the Byzantine period Orthodox Jews kept living in Capharnaum alongside Christians who in the meantime increased considerably. The sharp increase of Christians among the inhabitants of Capharnaum is clearly documented by archaeological findings; in fact, in any sector of the village so far excavated, most of the houses were provided with imported bowls having stamped crosses.

In the early seventh century many houses were abandoned and left to ruin, suggesting that the old population of Capharnaum, i.e. Jews and Christians alike, left the site. The fact that in the early Arab period both the synagogue and the octagonal church were abandoned seems to suggest that the newcomers were predominantly Moslems.

31

# THE SYNAGOGUES

## THE FOURTH CENTURY A.D. SYNAGOGUE

### 1. Description

The monumental synagogue covering an impressive area was built in the physical centre of the town and was delimited on the four sides by streets.

In striking contrast to the private houses of black basalt stones, the synagogue was built almost entirely with white limestone blocks brought from quarries several miles away, the heaviest reaching almost four tons. The decorative elements (lintels, cornices, capitals etc.) leave the visitors spellbound.

According to Robinson, "for expense, and labour and ornament, the edifice surpasses any thing we have yet seen in Palestine". The synagogue is indeed "one of the most satisfying places to visit in all Palestine" (Albright).

The restoration of the synagogue, initiated by Fr. Orfali in 1922-1925 and continued by Fr. Corbo since 1969, provides an idea of the original splendour of the monument. In 1984 all the architectural elements have been gathered according to typological and functional criteria and they were carefully catalogued by Fr. E. Alliata. This preliminary work will provide more solid ground for an ideal reconstruction of the complex. For the time being, we offer the hypothetical reconstruction suggested by Watzinger.

The synagogue is made up of four units, namely the prayer hall, the

30. Lintel of the synagogue (main entrance to the prayer hall).
31. Prayer hall of the synagogue.
32. The synagogue from the E courtyard.

## 33. General plan of the 4th century A.D. synagogue.

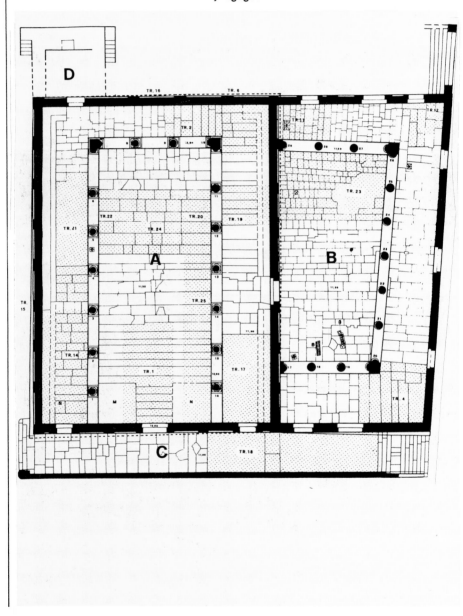

eastern courtyard, the southern porch, and a side-room near the outer NW corner of the prayer hall.

The prayer hall, with the facade facing S, i. e. toward Jerusalem, is rectangular in ground plan, the inner sides measuring 23 m from N to S, and 17.28 m from E to W. A U-shaped stylobate divides the spacious central nave from the E, W and N aisles. Two rows of stone benches were set along the peripheral walls of the E and W aisles. Strangely enough, the N aisle did not have benches. The inner walls of the prayer hall were decorated with painted plaster and stuccoes. The focal point of the prayer hall was in the Jerusalem-oriented wall of the central nave; prayers were said facing the three openings of the facade. The scrolls of the Law to be read during the religious gatherings were permanently kept on this S side of the central nave. However, two stages can be detected. In the original stage, dating back to the construction of the synagogue, two "bemas" were built on both sides of the central entrance. Only their square foundations (2.90 m) are preserved. Similar "aediculae" have been found in other synagogues, namely in Sardis, Nabratein, Beth Shearim, Gush Alav. In a second stage, a more sophisticated "teba" was built in the same place, covering the whole width of the central nave.

The interpretation of the side-room near the NW corner of the prayer hall is controversial. The subsidiary chamber, built entirely with basalt stone blocks, belongs to the original stage of the white synagogue. It is entered only from the prayer hall through a doorway still "in situ", while along the outer walls two flights of steps are partially preserved. Some scholars assumed in the past that the side room was meant as a shelter for the Holy Ark which was brought out to the S side of the central nave only during the worship service. This interpretation, however, is no longer tenable after the discovery of the two symmetrical "aediculae" on both sides of the central entrance. The outer steps are generally interpreted as leading to the upper gallery for women. The existence, however, of such matroneum is still an open question which perhaps can be solved only after all the architectural elements of the synagogue are properly analysed.

36. Stucco from the synagogue.
37. Lintel with the Ark of the Law.

38. Console with palm-tree.

39. Greek inscription from the synagogue:
HEROD (the son) OF MONIMOS
AND JUSTOS (his) SON TOGETHER WITH
THEIR CHILDREN ERECTED
THIS COLUMN.

The prayer hall directly communicated with the eastern courtyard through a doorway. The central space of the trapezoidal courtyard was surrounded on three sides by a roofed portico; three doorways were set on the N wall and two on the S side. The three large openings along the E side are not doorways but windows, since they are much higher than the street level. On the stone slabs of the pavement several "games" are still preserved. Most probably they were etched only in the Arab period, when the synagogue went out of use. In fact the same "games" were found in the prayer hall and even in some stones of the main walls of the synagogue.

Along the S flank of the prayer hall and of the E court a porch was set with two flights of steps on the E and W ends. Another large staircase was located near the NE corner of the court.

# 2. History of the Synagogue

Recent excavations clarified the long history of the white synagogue: (1) the prayer hall and the NW side room were built in the late fourth century A.D.; (2) the E court was added later on and was completed after the mid-fifth century A.D.; at the same time the S porch was remodelled; (3) the synagogue remained in use through the whole Byzantine period and was abandoned during the seventh century A.D.; (4) after the final abandonment, several stones of the synagogue were reused in some private dwellings of the Arab period or reduced to mortar.

As for the original dating of the white synagogue, both Wilson and Orfali still believed that the precious remains were nothing less than the famous first century synagogue. To the contrary most scholars in the past, following Watzinger's theory, dated the white synagogue to be around the late second-early third century A.D. All these theories, based on stylistic and historical considerations are no longer tenable. Archaeological data gathered in many seasons of excavations since 1969 make it clear that the prayer hall was built in the late fourth century A.D. These revolutionary conclusions are based on more than 30,000 Late Roman coins and on the study of the pottery.

41

41. Some Late Roman coins from the synagogue.
42. Lintel of the synagogue.

Even before our recent excavations, several scholars had suggested that the famous first century synagogue visited by Jesus was most probably buried under the monumental white synagogue. Albright, for example, lamented: "It is a pity that no earlier remains have yet been discovered. It is by no means unlikely that there are foundations of an older synagogue under the ruins of the third-century (sic) synagogue of Capernaum, but no one is likely to pull down this splendid structure on the chance of finding inferior remains beneath it". What Albright deemed as an improbable and formidable task was indeed accomplished by Fran-ciscan archaeologists. Starting from 1969, Fr. Corbo and the writer exposed all the areas surrounding the white synagogue, and cut several trenches inside the building in order to clarify and study earlier remains hidden under the fourth century synagogue.

The main results of this long and painstaking research are as follows: (1) The white synagogue was built upon an artificial podium. (2) The podium or raised platform was not built on virgin soil but upon an area of the village. After removing both the thick layer of mortar underneath the stone slabs of the pavements and the artificial fill of the platform, sev-

## 43. Structures predating the fourth century synagogue.

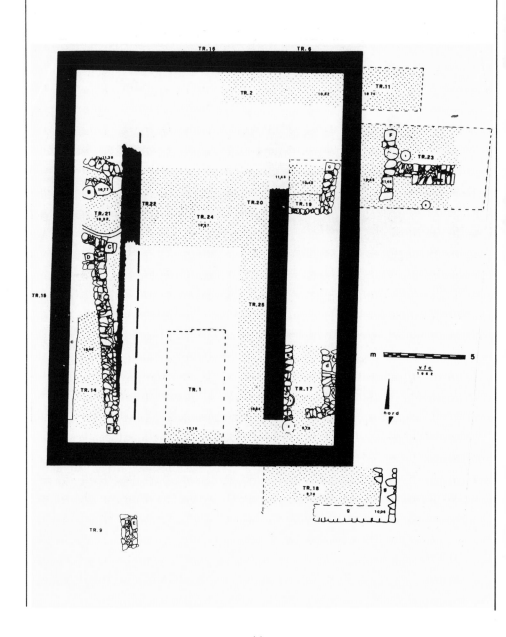

eral structures were found dating back to the Hellenistic and Roman periods. Actually in trench 21 even a Late Bronge Age structure of the 13th century was exposed. (3) These remains consist of superimposed stone pavements, basalt stone walls, doorways, staircases, water-channels and fire places. Though a complete plan of these structures is still impossible, due to the limits of the trenches, it is clear that these elements belong to private houses. They were found imbedded in the areas of the side aisles of the prayer hall, in the area of the porch, and finally in the area of the E court. (4) A quite different picture emerged from the trenches cut in the large area of the central nave of the prayer hall. Here in fact only a basalt stone pavement was traced dating back to the first century A.D. That pavement covered an older layer of occupation where pottery and some coins of the Hellenistic period were found. Both Fr. Corbo and the writer agree that the very large stone pavement of the first century A.D. uncovered beneath the central nave of the white synagogue does belong to the long-looked for synagogue built by the Roman centurion and visited by Jesus.

Several reasons are given for this identification. To start with, the area of the first century stone pavement is

46. Excavations in the central nave of the synagogue:
A. Stylobate of the 4th century A.D. synagogue.
B. The Basalt Stone Wall.
C. First century A.D. stone pavement.

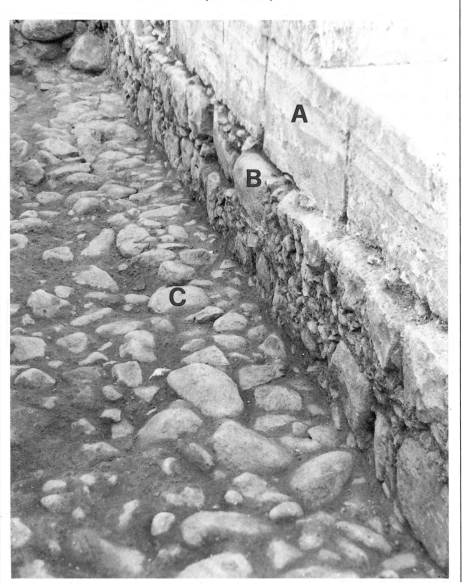

47. Excavations along the porch
of the synagogue.

too large to be interpreted as belonging to a private house, and is therefore better understood as the remains of a public building. It is reasonable to interpret that public building as a synagogue. It is well known in fact that religious structures were normally rebuilt in the same sacred area through the centuries. In the specific case of Capharnaum, the presence of an earlier synagogue would better explain why the fourth century Jewish community of the village chose this very spot to raise the monumental white synagogue in spite of the fact that the chosen area was extremely close to a Christian shrine. Finally, this identification takes into account the fact that pilgrims (as Egeria) located the first century synagogue in the area of the white synagogue. We must turn now to a second element, i. e. to what we called the "basalt stone wall" and see if that structure might be also related to the first century synagogue. The "basalt stone wall" was found both under the peripheral walls of the fourth century prayer hall and under the stylobate. However the "basalt stone wall" is

48. W flank of the synagogue
after the excavations.

continuous in the first case, whereas under the stylobate is discontinuous or in some cases completely missing. Both Fr. Corbo and the writer agree on one important point: the "basalt stone wall" predates the white synagogue and is better understood as belonging to an earlier synagogue. In other words, the "basalt stone wall" was simply reused as the foundation of the white synagogue, but effectively was not simply a foundation, but the remaining wall of an older synagogue. This interpretation becomes plausible as soon as the "basalt stone wall" is carefully studied both in relation to the foundations of the E court and to the walls of the prayer hall.

To start with, the foundations of E court were built independently: they simply abut to the "basalt stone wall". Secondly, they are made up of beautiful stone blocks carefully executed and with an excellent refinement of the courses, while the courses of the "basalt stone wall" are inferior both in quality and in finish. Why this striking difference of foundations? Why did the courtyard which was a secondary unit rest upon excellent foundations, while much poorer foundations were found for the prayer hall which was the most important part of the fourth century synagogue? The only answer we can provide is this: the prayer hall simply reused as foundations the walls of a pre-existing

building, while the foundation of the E court was built anew much later. This conclusion is strengthened when we analyse the interrelation between the "basalt stone wall" and the courses of the prayer hall resting upon it. As we have said, the "basalt stone wall" is conspicuously discontinuous beneath the stylobates of the prayer hall. What is worse, the N stylobate of the prayer hall rests upon a shaky fill and in that area the "basalt stone wall" is completely missing. Secondly, there is a shift in axiality between the "basalt stone wall" and the outer walls of the prayer hall. Finally, since the "basalt stone wall" sloped from N to S, the builders of the white synagogue had to taper all the stones of the first course in the opposite direction, i. e. from S to N, and, furthermore, they used pebbles to fill the undulant top of the "basalt stone wall". For all these reasons we must conclude that the "basalt stone wall" belongs to a synagogue predating the white synagogue. What is the relation between the "basalt stone wall" and the first century stone pavement found in the central nave? The director of the excavations believes that both elements belong to the first century synagogue. Another possibility is in my opinion that the "basalt stone wall" constitutes an intermediate stage between the first century synagogue and the white synagogue of the late fourth century A.D.

# THE INSULA SACRA

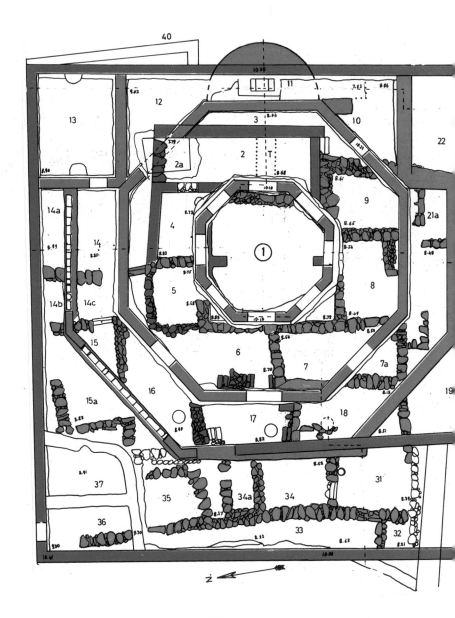

## 50. General plan of the Insula Sacra:
### Level 1 (red): Private houses of the 1st century B.C.
### Level 2 (green): The 4th century A.D. Domus-Ecclesia.
### Level 3 (blue): The mid-5th A.D. Octagonal Church.

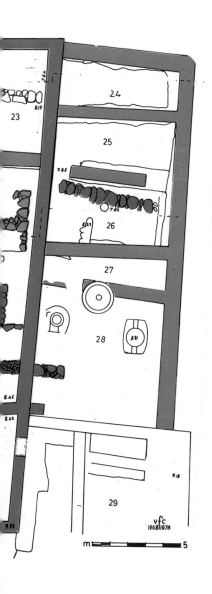

The house of St. Peter, often mentioned by the Synoptic Gospels in relation to the activity of Jesus in Capharnaum, and recorded later on by pilgrims, was rediscovered in 1968 under the foundations of the octagonal church some 30 m south of the synagogue. The history of that house where Jesus lived, can be summarised as follows: (1) the house was built in the Late Hellenistic period: (2) in the late first century A.D. it was changed into a "domus-ecclesia", i. e. became a house for religious gatherings; (3) in the fourth century A.D. the same "domus-ecclesia" was enlarged and was set apart from the rest of the town through an imposing enclosure wall; (4) in the second half of the fifth century A.D. an octagonal church was built upon the house of St. Peter and remained in use until the seventh century A.D.; (5) the identification of the house of St. Peter is based on the combination of archaeological data and literary sources which run side by side in a wonderful way.

The new church (of the Italian architect Ildo Avetta) was dedicated on June 29, 1990.

51

# 1. The Private Houses

The private houses of insula n. 1 (called by us insula sacra) follow the same pattern as the houses of the other living quarters of the village, i. e. are characterised by small roofed rooms clustering around large courtyards. The traditional house of St. Peter (room n. 1) was almost square in ground plan. The W wall, still preserved for more than a meter in height, measures 8.35 m in length.

The room was entered from a doorway partially preserved on the N flank near the NW corner. An L-shaped courtyard, entered from the E through a well preserved threshold, and provided with a staircase and with characteristic "terra refractaria" fire places, covered a conspicuous area of ca. 84 square meters.

The courtyard was shared not only by the traditional house of St. Peter, but by several other roofed rooms as well, suggesting that more than one family lived together around the same courtyard. The house of St. Peter was flanked on the E side by the main NS street of the village. There was an ad-

## 52. Isometric view of the Insula Sacra at the time of Jesus.

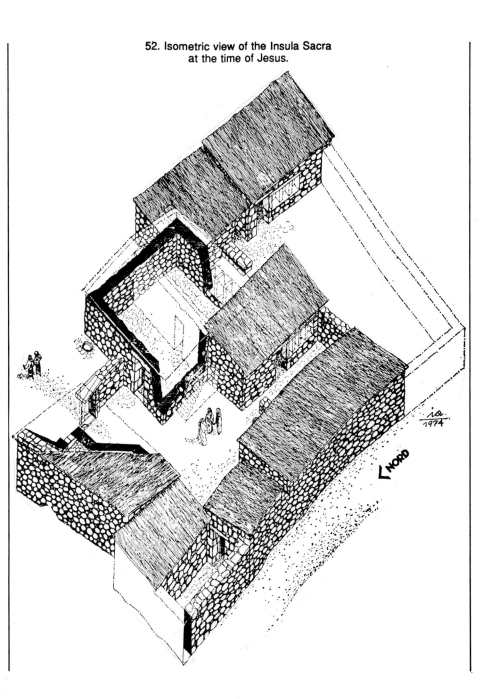

ditional open space between the street and the entrance to the L-shaped courtyard. More houses were traced in the S portion of the same insula. There again the open courtyards were the focal point of several roofed rooms. In ancient time the S houses of insula n. 1 were very close to the lake shore.

The insula sacra belongs to the original nucleus settlement of the Late Hellenistic period. The long period of unbroken occupation is evidenced by a sequence of at least three superimposed stone pavements. As a matter of fact, four superimposed stone pavements were found in a trench cut by us in the L-shaped

courtyard against the W wall of room n. 1. The lowest stone pavement with traces of a fire place gave only Hellenistic sherds. The first century stone pavement is the second from the bottom. Several trial trenches were dug also inside room n. 1 in order to check the history of that special room. Here too several superimposed layers of occupation were recorded, starting from the Late Hellenistic period. From the second century B.C. to the late first century A.D., the occupational layers are made up of straight horizontal lines of beaten earth mixed with daily life vessels, such as jars, cooking pots, bowls, lamps etc.

55. Soundings inside Room n. 1 of the House of Peter.

Above these earliest strata, something very unique was recorded: on the NE side of the room an area of ca. 12 square m was cleared, having a pavement of at least six superimposed layers of white plaster. Besides, some painted fragments of plaster, originally decorating the inner walls of that room were found. Last but not least, the only evidence of occupation was a good number of tiny little pieces of Herodian lamps; they were imbedded in the white plastered pavements. More Herodian lamps were found along the inner walls. The lamps can be dated typologically in the second half of the first century A.D. and certainly not later than the beginning of the second century.

The superimposed plastered pavements were kept scrupulously clean, contrarily to the previous strata; in fact no occupational soil was found between the thin layers of plaster. At the same time the almost complete absence of daily life vessels is striking.

It should be stressed that this is the only case in which a room with plastered pavements and walls has been found in Capharnaum, in spite of the fact that a very large portion of the ancient village has been brought to light.

The least we can say is that the traditional house of St. Peter (room n. 1) was used for community gatherings as early as the third quarter of the first century A.D. The religious and Christian character of those gatherings will be better understood in the light of the upper strata of the same room.

# 2. The Domus-Ecclesia

Following an unbroken sequence of occupation, the insula sacra underwent major changes in the late fourth century A.D. First of all, insula n. 1 was set apart from the rest of the village through the construction of an impressive enclosure wall encompassing a perimeter of 112.25 m. The area enclosed by the wall was roughly square in ground plan and was entered from two doorways respectively near the SW and NW corners of the enclosure wall. An additional screen wall in a NS direction departed from the SW entrance.

The construction of the enclosure wall brought about the destruction of some houses. At the same time room n. 1 became the focal point of the reshaped insula sacra and underwent significant changes. To start with, the inner space of room n. 1, measuring 5.80 by 6.45 m, received a new polychrome pavement. An arch spanning from N to S across the middle of the chamber was added in order to subdivide the space in two units. The N wall of the room was rebuilt, whereas the remaining three walls were left standing. A new roof made up of strong mortar replaced the old one. Finally an E atrium with white plastered pavement and a NE side-chamber were added. Both the inner walls and the newly built arch in the centre of the room were plastered.

It is significant that in due time the piers of the central arch received two superimposed coatings of painted plaster; whereas three successive layers are preserved along the old walls of the room. This observation leads us to the conclusion that the inner walls of room n. 1 were plastered at least once before the fourth century. This conclusion is in line with the palaeographic

58. Isometric view of the 4th century A.D.
Domus-Ecclesia.
59. Enclosure wall of the 4th century Domus-Ecclesia.

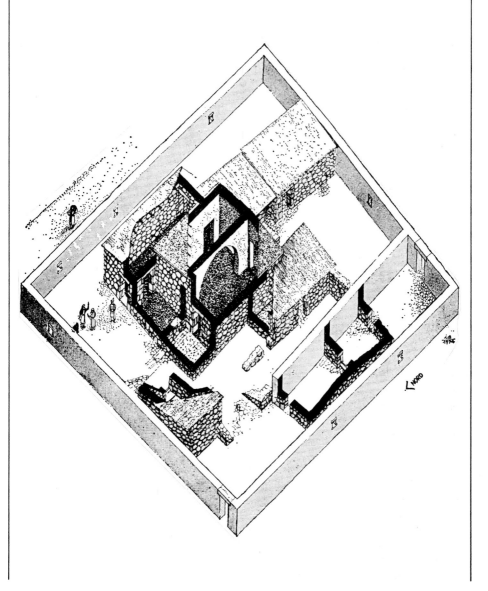

study of the graffiti the oldest of which are dated by Fr. Testa in the early third century A.D.

Different colours were used to decorate the plastered walls, namely red, pink, brick-red, yellow, dark brown, green, blue and white. The geometric decoration is made up of rectangular panels, lozenges, circles, floral crosses etc. Floral motifs are also recognisable, such as branches, small trees, flowers, figs and pomegranates. Apparently no human or animal representations were allowed.

Last but not least, several graffiti, monograms and symbols were found. The languages used in the graffiti are Greek (151 samples), Paleo-Estrangelo (13), Aramaic (9) and Latin (2).

This precious material was studied and published by Fr. E. Testa. Although the interpretation of the inscriptions is far from easy, due to the fragmentary and precarious state of preservation, yet some very important conclusions are beyond any reasonable doubt.

The Christian character of the domus-ecclesia is clearly vindicated. In fact the name and the monogram of Jesus occur in several graffiti. Jesus is called the Lord, Christ, the Most High, God. Some liturgical expressions, such as Amen, Kyrie eleison, etc. are also present. A fairly long inscription in Paleo-Estrangelo seems to refer to the Eucharist. The plurality of languages strongly suggests that the domus-ecclesia was visited not simply by local worshipers, but by pilgrims as well. On palaeographic grounds, the graffiti can be dated from the beginning of the third century to the early fifth century A.D. This conclusion, coupled with the late first century plastered pavements previously described, suggests that room n. 1 was changed into a domus-ec-

clesia by the first generations of Christians in Capharnaum.

The cult centered of course on the person of Jesus. Yet, it is not surprising to find some graffiti bearing the name of Peter. From the strictly archaeological point of view, the enlarged domus-ecclesia of the fourth century constitutes a unique discovery. It is a tripartite structure having the atrium to the E and the focal point to the W; furthermore the building is set apart from the rest of town by an enclosure wall. These basic elements are strongly reminiscent of the general plan of the Temple in Jerusalem. Such similarities cannot be interpreted as accidental, especially when we think that Christians from Jewish stock lived in Capharnaum in the first four centuries of the Christian era.

The fourth century domus-ecclesia was described by Egeria in these terms: "In Capharnaum autem ex domo apostolorum principis ecclesia facta est, cuius parietes usque hodie ita stant, sicut fuerunt", i. e. "The house of the prince of the Apostles (St. Peter) in Capharnaum was changed into a church; the walls, however, (of that house) are still standing as they were (in the past)". This precious passage of Egeria reached us through Petrus Diaconus (1137) and is important for several reasons. Egeria does not speak of a common church, but of a house changed into a church. To stress this point, Egeria underlines the fact that the walls of the old house were still standing as in the past. Secondly, this change of a private house into a place for religious gatherings took place in the past (facta est). Finally the house converted into a church was nothing less than the house of the prince of the Apostles, i. e. of Simon Peter. Nobody can miss the striking accuracy of Egeria's description in the light of our archaeological discoveries.

## 3. The Octagonal Church

In the second half of the fifth century a bold project was carried out in the area delimited by the fourth century enclosure wall, namely the domus-ecclesia and all the structures of the insula sacra were buried under a fill, and an octagonal church was erected on a raised level. The Byzan-tine church was built according to a pattern completely different from the previous domus-ecclesia. A small E apse marked the new orientation. In order to create a direct approach to the octagonal church, several private houses along the outer W side of the enclosure wall were dismantled. For the same purpose, the W portion of the enclosure wall was cut down to the average level of the mosaic floor of the church.

The plan of the church consist-ed of a small central octagon, of a

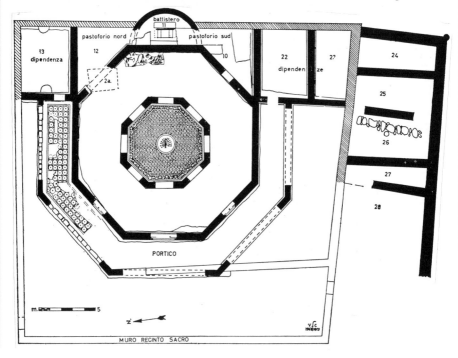

larger concentric octagon, and by an outer semi-octagon from which one could reach both the interior of the church and the E sacristies.

In a second phase a baptismal font was added in the middle of the E apse. The motif of a peacock, symbol of immortality, dominated the mosaic floor of the central octagon.

The foundations were built with basalt stones and strong mortar; whereas the superstructure was raised with white limestone blocks.

This bold project is to be attributed to the Gentile-Christians who by that time were strong enough to contrast the supremacy of the old Jewish-Christian community of Capharnaum. It is well known that the relations between these two branches of Christianity were far from smooth; very often the Jewish Christians met strong opposition both from Orthodox Jews and from Gentile-Christians. Yet, the Gentile-Christians were not afraid of preserving the sacrality of several Jewish-Christian shrines. In the specific case of Capharnaum the physical links between the buried house of St. Peter and the superimposed octagon are striking.

Actually the planning of a church of octagonal shape was dictated by a twofold preoccupation; it was meant to preserve the fourth century enclosure wall, and especially to indicate the exact location of St. Peter's house. As a matter of fact, the foundations of the central octagon were set exactly upon the walls of that special square room (room n. 1) attributed to the house of St. Peter. It is true that pilgrims were no longer able to see that venerated house buried under the central octagon. Yet the tradition about the house of St. Peter was not lost. A pilgrim from Piacenza who visited Capharnaum around 570 A.D. wrote: "Item venimus in Capharnaum in domo beati Petri, quae est modo basilica", i. e.: "We came to Capharnaum in St. Peter's house, which at present is a basilica".

66a. Friezes from the synagogue.

# CAPHARNAUM AND
# THE GOSPELS

## 1.
### Capharnaum "the Town of Jesus"

The rediscovered remains of Capharnaum help us to set several passages of the Gospels in the human and physical context of that site. We learn from the Gospels that Jesus left Nazareth and settled in Capharnaum (Mt 4:12) which in some way became "his own town" (Mt 9:1). Actually Capharnaum much more than Nazareth offered to Jesus a twofold advantage as far as his mes-

sianic activity was concerned. First-ly, Capharnaum was a crossroad of primary importance, being along the Beth-shan — Damascus highway; whereas Nazareth was a mountainous and isolated hamlet. Secondly, Capharnaum was sufficiently apart from the big centres and especially from Tiberias where Herod Antipas had set his capital. In that way Jesus was able to spread his messianic message to many persons without running too soon into trouble with the political and religious leaders. In contrast to Nazareth, the population of Capharnaum was highly stratified: fishermen, farmers, artisans, mer-

chants, publicans etc. Lived in the same village, but apparently without any strident economical inequality. Even the relations between the inhabitants of Capharnaum and the Romans were surprisingly cordial. It was a Roman centurion who built the synagogue for the Jewish community, while the elders of the village reciprocated in kindness and pleaded earnestly with Jesus asking him to heal the centurion's servant (Lc 7:1-10). All in all, the inhabitants of Capharnaum were hard workers, parsimonious and open-minded; to those people Jesus addressed himself while in Capharnaum and from the same community Jesus chose many of his apostles either among fishermen (Peter, Andrew, James, John) or publicans (Matthew).

## 2. The first disciples

"...Leaving Nazareth he went and settled in Capharnaum, a lakeside town on the borders of Zebulun and Naphtali. In this way the prophecy of Isaiah was to be fulfilled: Land of Zebulun! Land of Naphtali! Way of the sea on the far side of Jordan, Galilee of the nations! The people that lived in darkness has seen a great light; on those who dwell in the land and shadow of death a light has dawned. From that moment Jesus began his preaching with the message, 'Repent, for the kingdom of heaven is close at hand'.

As he was walking by the Sea of Galilee, he saw two brothers, Simon, who was called Peter, and his brother Andrew; they were making a cast in the lake with their net, for they were fishermen. And he said to them, 'Follow me and I will make you fishers of men'. And they left their nets at once and followed him. Going on from there he saw another pair of brothers, James son of Zebedee and his brother John; they were in their boat with their father Zebedee, mending their nets, and he called them. At once, leaving the boat and their father, they followed him" (Mt 4:12-22).

"He went out again to the shore of the lake, and all the people came to him, and he taught them. As he was walking on he saw Levi the son of Alphaeus, sitting by the customs house, and he said to him, 'Follow me'. And he got up and followed him.

When Jesus was at dinner in his house, a number of tax collectors and sinners were also sitting at the table with Jesus and his disciples, for there were many of them among his followers. When the scribes of the Pharisee party saw him eating with sinners and tax collectors, they said to his disciples, 'Why does he eat with tax collectors and sinners?' When Jesus heard this he said to them, 'It is not the healthy who need the doctor, but the sick. I did not come to call the virtuous, but sinners' (Mc 2:13).

### 3. The house of Simon Peter

We have shown that the Christian community of Capharnaum paid a special attention to the house of Simon Peter. That house became very soon "the house" of the followers of Jesus, i. e. a domus-ecclesia. As a matter of fact, the rediscovered house of Peter is the first example of a domus-ecclesia in the Christian world. The special reasons for this choice can be found in the Gospels. It was Jesus himself who had chosen that house as his home in Capharnaum. In the same way that Capharnaum became "the town of Jesus", Peter's house could be called rightly "the house of Jesus". When we keep in mind the proverbial conciseness of the Gospels, we are immediately struck by their numerous references to the house of Peter. Here are some pertinent passages.

"On leaving the synagogue, he went with James and John straight to the house of Simon and Andrew. Now Simon's mother-in-law had gone to bed with fever, and they told him about her straightaway. He went to her, took her by the hand and helped her up. And the fever left her and she began to wait on them. That evening,

after sunset, they brought to him all who were sick and those who were possessed by devils. The whole town came crowding round the door, and he cured many who were suffering from diseases of one kind or another; he also cast out many devils, but he would not allow them to speak, because they knew who he was" (Mc 1:29-34; cfr. Mt 8:14-17; Lc 4:38-41).

There are several details which recent archaeological discoveries can clarify in a concrete way. The house visited by Jesus was only some 30 m south of the synagogue. It was a large house precisely in fact that it consisted of several roofed rooms clustering around a spacious courtyard. We are therefore not surprised when we read in the Gospels that the same house was shared by three families, namely by the families of Peter, of his brother Andrew and of Peter's mother-in-law. Actually this was the standard pattern of the private houses in the living quarters of Capharnaum. We read that "the whole town came crowding round the door". This detail clearly suggests that a large space was available in front of the house. This is the case indeed. The rediscovered house was along the main NS street of the village and an additional open space was between the spacious street and the doorway leading to the courtyard of the house. "When they reached Capharnaum, the collectors of the half-shekel came to Peter and said, 'Does your master not pay the half-shekel?' 'Oh yes' he replied, and went into the house. But before he could speak, Jesus said, 'Simon, what is your opinion? From whom do the kings of the earth take toll or tribute? From their sons or from foreigners?' And when he replied, 'From foreigners', Jesus said, 'Well then, the sons are exempt. However, so as not to offend these people, go to the lake and cast a hook; take the first fish that bites, open its mouth and there you will find a shekel; take it to them for me and for you' (Mt 17 :24-27).

Only Matthew, who was previously a tax collector, relates this story. Peter is described as the intermediary between the tax collectors and Jesus. Apparently he was ready to pay both for himself and for Jesus. It is Jesus however who solves the tribute for both. The whole passage hints that Jesus was a guest of Peter, and as

such was considered as a member of Peter's family. For this reason, Peter and Jesus are put together in fact of taxes.

"When he returned to Capharnaum some time later, word went round that he was at home; and so many people collected that there was no room left, even in front of the door. He was preaching the word to them when some people came bringing him a paralytic carried by four men, but as the crowd made it impossible to get the man to him, they stripped the roof over the place where Jesus was; and when they had made an opening, they lowered the stretcher on which the paralytic lay..." (Mc 2:1-4; cfr. Mt 9:1-18; Lc 5:17-26).

The mention of the people gathered even in front of the door is a literary reference to Mc 1:33. The Greek expression "en oikoi" can be translated either as in a house, or at home. The second rendering is here recommended. In other words, the healing of the paralytic took place in Peter's house where Jesus lived. The lowering of the paralytic from the stripped roof is not strange at all in the context of the rediscovered living quarters of Capharnaum, where indeed the one storey rooms were covered by light roofs reached through a flight of steps from the courtyard.

72

71. Stone steps and oven in the courtyard
of St. Peter's House.

"He went home again, and once more such a crowd collected that they could not even have a meal. When his relatives heard of this, they set out to take charge of him, convinced he was out of his mind... "His mother and brothers now arrived and, standing outside, sent in a message asking for him. A crowd was sitting round him at the time the message was passed to him, 'Your mother and brothers are outside asking for you'. He replied, 'Who are my mother and my brothers?' And looking round at those sitting in a circle about him, he said, 'Here are my mother and my brothers. Anyone who does the will of God, that person is my brother and sister and mother' " (Mc 3:20-21 and 31-35; cfr. Mt 12:46-50; Lc 8:10-21).

The passage depicts two families of Jesus, i. e. his relatives waiting outside, and his followers sitting around him in the house. In the redactional stage of St. Marc the contrast between those who are outside and those who are inside the house, betrays ecclesial-christological dimensions, meaning those who are inside or outside the Christian community. In some way the house of Jesus in Capharnaum i.e. the house of Peter, receives here the connotations of a domus-ecclesia.

## 4. Jairus and the Roman centurion

Besides the house of Simon Peter, three more houses are explicitly mentioned in the Gospels, namely the house of Matthew, where Jesus dined with many tax collectors (Mc 2:15-17); the house of the synagogue official Jairus, the little daughter of whom was brought to life by Jesus (Mc 5:35-43); and the house of the Roman centurion (Lc 7:1-10). There is no way to tell where those houses can be found; and this remark applies also to the house of the apostles James and John who for sure were stationed in Capharnaum (Mc 1:19-20). Apparently their location did not interest the Christian community of Capharnaum or at most was soon forgotten. It is not impossible that some of these houses were indeed found by us in the large area so far excavated, but only the house of Peter has been identified.

### a. The daughter of Jairus raised to life

"When Jesus had crossed again in the boat to the other side, a large crowd gathered round him and he stayed by the lakeside. Then one of the synagogue officials came up, Jairus by name, and seeing him, fell at his feet and pleaded with him earnestly, saying, 'My little daughter is desperately sick. Do come and lay your hands on her to make her better and save her life'. Jesus went with him and a large crowd followed him; they were pressing all round him...

... While he was still speaking some people arrived from the house of the synagogue official to say, 'Your daughter is dead: why put the Master to any further trouble?' But Jesus had overheard this remark of theirs and he said to the official, 'Do not be afraid; only have faith'. And he allowed no one to go with him except Peter and James and John the brother of James. So they came to the official's house and Jesus noticed all the commotion, with people weeping and wailing unrestrainedly. He went in and said to them, 'Why all this commotion and crying? The child is not dead, but asleep'. But they laughed at him. So he turned them all out and, taking with him the child's father and mother and his companions, he went into the place where the child lay. And taking the child by the hand he said to her, 'Talitha, kum!' which means, 'Little girl, I tell you to get up'. The little girl got up at once and began to walk about, for she was twelve years old. At this they were overcome with astonishment, and he ordered them strictly not to let anyone know about it, and told them to give her something to eat" (Mc 5:21-23, 35-43)

### b. Jesus cures the centurion's servant

"When he had come to the end of all he wanted the people to ear, he went into Capharnaum. A centurion there had a servant, a favourite of his, who was sick and near to death. Having heard about Jesus he sent some Jewish elders to him to ask him to come and heal his servant. When they came to Jesus they pleaded earnestly with him. 'He deserves this of you' they said 'because he is friendly towards our people; in fact, he is the one who built the synagogue'. So Jesus went with them, and was not very far from the house when the centurion sent word to him by some friends: 'Sir', he said 'do not put yourself to trouble; because I am not worthy to have you under my roof; and for this same reason I did not presume to come to you myself; but give the word and let my servant be cured. For I am under authority myself, and have soldiers under me; and I say to one man: Go, and he goes; to another: Come here, and he comes; to my servant: Do this, and he does it'. When Jesus heard these words, he was astonished at him and, turning round, said to the crowd following him, 'I tell you, not even in Israel have I found faith like this'. And when the messengers got back to the house they found the servant in perfect health" (Lc 7:1-10).

# 5. Jesus in the Synagogue

Only one public building, namely the synagogue built by the Roman centurion (Lc 7:5) is mentioned in the Gospels. Of course the synagogue was the hearth of the Jewish community and Jesus visited it several times. In that synagogue of Capharnaum Jesus preached and performed some miracles. We read in Mc 1:21-28: "They went as far as Capharnaum, and as soon as the sabbath came he went to the synagogue and began to teach. And his teaching made a deep impression on them because, unlike the scribes, he taught them with authority. "In their synagogue just then there was a man possessed by an unclean spirit and he shouted, 'What do you want with us, Jesus of Nazareth? Have you come to destroy us? I know who you are: the Holy One of God'. But Jesus said sharply, 'Be quiet! Come out of him!' and the unclean spirit threw the man into convulsion and with a loud cry went out of him. The people were so astonished that they started asking each other what it all meant. 'Here is a teaching that is new' they said 'and with authority behind it: he gives orders even to unclean spirits and they obey him'. And his reputation rapidly spread everywhere, through all the surrounding Galilean countryside".

It was in the same synagogue that Jesus promised the Eucharist. The evangelist St. John devoted a long chapter to the discourse of Jesus on the bread of life (John 6:22-71). Let us read only some passages. "I tell you most solemnly, it was not Moses who gave you bread from heaven, it is my Father who gives you the bread from heaven, the true bread; for the bread of God is that which comes down from heaven and gives life to the world... I am the bread of life. He who comes to me will never be hungry; he who believes in me will never thirst... I am the living bread that comes down from heaven, so that a man may eat it and not die. I am the living bread which has come down from heaven. Anyone who eats this bread will live for ever, and the bread that I shall give is my flesh, for the life of the world... I tell you most solemnly, if you do not eat the flesh of the Son of man and drink his blood, you will not have life in you. Anyone who does eat my flesh and drink my blood has eternal life and I shall raise him up on the last day... He taught this doctrine at Capharnaum, in the synagogue".

Some remains of the first century synagogue have been found in the same area where the Jewish community of the late fourth century A.D. built the monumental white synagogue. Strangely enough, only Egeria mentions the synagogue of Capharnaum; whereas Jewish sources are inexplicably silent about this splendid building which for sure is the queen of the Galilean synagogues.

 **6.** **The calming
of the storm**

"Then he got into the boat followed by his disciples. Without warning a storm broke the lake, so violent that the waves were breaking right over the boat. But he was asleep. So they went to him and woke him saying, 'Save us, Lord, we are going down!' And he said to them, 'Why are you so frightened, you men of little faith?' And with that he stood up and rebuked the winds and the sea; and all was calm again. The men were astounded and said, 'Whatever kind of man is this? Even the winds and the sea obey him'" (Mt 8:23-27).

"Directly after this (i. e. after the first miracle of the loaves) he made the disciples get into the boat and go on ahead to the other side while he would send the crowds away. After sending the crowds away he went up into the hills by himself to pray. When evening came, he was there alone, while the boat, by now far out on the lake, was battling with a heavy sea, for there was a head-wind. In the fourth watch of the night he went towards them, walking on the lake, and when the disciples saw him walking on the lake they were terrified. 'It is a ghost' they said, and cried out in fear.

## 72. Violent storm at Capharnaum.

But at once Jesus called out to them, saying, 'Courage! It is I! Do not be afraid'. It was Peter who answered, 'Lord,' he said 'if it is you, tell me to come to you across the water'. 'Come' said Jesus. Then Peter got out of the boat and started walking towards Jesus across the water, but as soon as he felt the force of the wind, he took fright and began to sink. 'Lord! Save me!' he cried. Jesus put out his hand at once and held him. 'Man of little faith,' he said, 'why did you doubt?' And as they got into the boat the wind dropped. The men in the boat bowed down before him and said, 'Truly, you are the Son of God" (Mt 14:22-33).

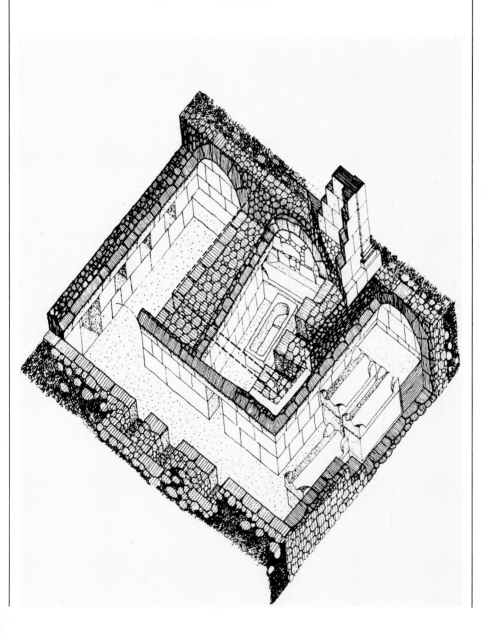

## 73. The Roman Mausoleum.

# THE ROMAN MAUSOLEUM

The old cemetery lies on the northern side of the town, some 200 m from the synagogue. An imposing mausoleum, partly known to the explorers of the XIX century, was fully excavated in 1976/77. The mausoleum was made up of two complementary structures, namely of an open air monument (nephesh) and of an underground burial place (hypogeum). Both structures were constructed with highly polished stone blocks: limestone was used for the nephesh and basalt for the hypogeum. While the open air monument is in a very bad condition of preservation (only the foundations are still in place), the hypogeum is almost perfectly preserved. The main burial chamber, which lies under the nephesh, is flanked on three sides by a corridor. The entrance to the hypogeum was on the east side, near the NE corner. Both the corridor and the central burial chamber have an arched roof. Three white limestone sarcophagi were found in the western corridor, and two more in the main burial chamber. Besides, eight kokhim for ossuaries were located along the outer walls of the corridor and of the central chamber. The tomb was plundered anciently. It was probably built in the first two centuries of the Christian era.

# CONCLUSION

Recent excavations shed a new light on the biblical site of Capharnaum. A large portion of the living quarters were exposed; and the public buildings, namely the synagogue and the octagonal church, were set again in their physical and historical contexts.

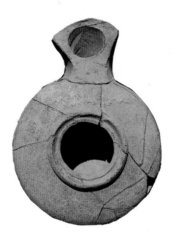

A complex picture emerged. At first glance the two public buildings appear out of proportion to the needs of a village and in striking contrast to the unsophisticated living quarters. Apparently the sober inhabitants of Capharnaum spared no effort to stress the absolute pre-eminence of spiritual values.

Visitors are also puzzled in finding a Jewish synagogue and a Christian shrine side by side. To be sure, the location of the two public buildings was dictated by the preoccupation of preserving the sacrality of both sites; the octagonal church in fact was built in order to perpetuate the exact location of St. Peter's house; and the late fourth century white synagogue rose on the remains of older synagogues.

Even more striking was our dating of the white synagogue in the late fourth century A.D. Some scholars found it unbelievable that such a monumental synagogue could be built under Christian emperors. Fortunately our excavations prompted new research concerning the monumental synagogues of Galilee. It turned out that this type of synagogue was still erected as late as in the sixth century A.D., as it is the case for the Nabratein synagogue. In short, many theories both in archaeological and historical fields fell apart after our investigation of ancient Capharnaum. Of course our discoveries were of great interest both to Scripture scholars and to those who are concerned with the early stage of Christianity.

Finally the unearthed remains are by now an open book for any visitors and pilgrims who come to this biblical site for a personal contact with the town of Jesus.

74. Herodian lamp from St. Peter's House.
75. General view of Capharnaum.

## SELECTED BIBLIOGRAPHY

KOHL H.-WATZINGER C., *Antike Synagogen in Galiläa*, Leipzig 1916.

ORFALI G., *Capharnaüm et ses ruines, d'après les fouilles accomplies à Tell-Houm par la Custodie Franciscaine de Terre Sainte (1905-1921)*, Paris 1922.

CORBO V., *Cafarnao*. Vol. I. *Gli Edifici della città*, Jerusalem 1975.

LOFFREDA S., *Cafarnao*. Vol. II. *La Ceramica*, Jerusalem 1974.

SPIJKERMAN A., *Cafarnao*. Vol. III. *Catalogo delle monete della città*, Jerusalem 1975.

TESTA E., *Cafarnao*. Vol. IV. *I graffiti della Casa di San Pietro*, Jerusalem 1972.

TZAFERIS V. ET ALII, *Excavations of Capernaum. I: 1978-1982*, Winola Lake, Indiana 1989.

# APPENDIX

## ST. PETER'S MEMORIAL

The new Memorial upon the traditional House of St. Peter was built by the Franciscan Custody of the Holy Land in order to shelter the archaeological remains of the Insula Sacra, and to make the same ruins more accessible to the visitors. The inside of the edifice is primarely reserved to religious services.

The Memorial was planned by the Italian architect Ildo Avetta. The main bulk of the building, which is hovering over the remains of the House of Simon Peter the fisherman, conveys in some way the image of a boat. The same idea is suggested by the wall decorations made up of stylised fish, waves and nets.

The four wooden panels inside the church are the work of the artists Raoul Vistoli (the Blessed Virgin entering the House of Peter, and St. Peter on a boat) and of Giovanni Dragoni (the Crucifixion and Jesus in the House of Peter). More panels are expected to embellish the interior surfaces of the Memorial. The mosaic of the altar (of Enzo Rossi) combines the biblical theme of the manna in the desert and of the multiplication of loaves. Some passages of the fourth Gospel relating the famous speech on the bread of life, made by Jesus in the synagogue of Capharnaum, are engraved on the walls of the presbytery. The central tabernacle (of Igino Legnaghi) reproduces the biblical taw letter. The artistic bronze railing (of Tavani) around the central oculus of the Memorial and along the entrance staircase, is a combination of Christian symbols.

The daring and ultra-modern project of Ildo Avetta entailed lengthy and complex studies conducted by the engineer Cesare Pocci and by many specialists of the Israeli Technion. The execution, through the Israeli building contracting company Solel Bonneh was supervised by the Engineer Anis Sruji of Nazareth.

The Memorial was dedicated by Card. Lourdusami on June 29th, 1990. That date was engraved on the plinths of the facade: BEATO PETRO APOSTOLO - A.D. MC-MXC DICATUM. (Dedicated to the blessed apostle Peter on June 29, 1990). In that memorable occasion the Holy Father John Paul II sent a special message, part of which has been engraved on both sides of the entrance.

The ancient texts of Egeria and of the Placentinus, together with the new dedicatory inscription, stress the continuity of the Christian tradition on this holy place which was at the same time the house of Peter, the house of Jesus, and the cradle of Christianity.

77. Some objects of the time of Jesus.